How
THE COMMUNIST MANIFESTO
Threatens Our Freedom Today

by Arthur R. Thompson

Published by
The John Birch Society
Appleton, Wisconsin

Published by
The John Birch Society
770 N. Westhill Boulevard
Appleton, Wisconsin 54914
www.JBS.org

Cover Design by Lindsey McConnell

Library of Congress Control Number: 2024940510
International Standard Book Number (ISBN): 978-1-881919-22-3

Printed in the United States of America

Table of Contents

Introduction

This book explains how *The Communist Manifesto* threatens our freedom today. The *Manifesto* was written primarily by Karl Marx, but with a good deal of help from his collaborator, Frederick Engels. While most of it deals with human nature, which never changes, it must be looked at today in light of many changes which have occurred over the last one and a half centuries since it was published and which have had their effect on government and society.

Since it deals with human nature, though, it still serves as a primer for the communist movement around the word. Other communist primers have been written, published, and widely distributed, such as the "Little Red Book" of Mao Tse-tung and a library full of books by Marxist leaders, professors, etc. There have also been other works by Marx himself, but the *Manifesto* is still the prime primer, and all communist countries, whether in Europe, Asia, or South America, still fly banners bearing the image of Marx, harking back to the *visible origins* of communism.

Another reason we should be interested in this small book today is that it has been called "The most widely read political pamphlet in the history of the world." This is because it has been promoted so much over the years by the growing communist organization.

The *Manifesto* is a very valuable look into the minds of the leadership of the conspirators who fomented the revolutions of 1848 and 1849 in Europe. Conspirators? In prefaces to later editions of the *Manifesto*, Engels revealed that indeed it was a secret society behind the communist movement. In other words, a conspiracy — which we will elaborate on in Chapter One.

Why should Americans be concerned with a book written so many years ago? We have already provided two reasons: It still serves as the basis for communism around the world, and it continues in widespread circulation. For a third reason, the conspiracy mentioned by Engels has purged knowledge of the influence of the communist movement from the American mind and American history in the last several decades.

American history? Yes. As an example of this, did you know that Karl Marx, due to the growing membership and influence of communism in the United States, moved the headquarters of the Communist International to New York City in 1872?

If you didn't know this, you might ask yourself why.

This influence in America was so great that two out of the ten major steps for communizing a country outlined in *The Communist Manifesto* were established into law in the United States just after the turn of the 20th century: the income tax and the Federal Reserve, or national bank (although a great deal of effort has been made to convince people that it is *not* a bank.) Other provisions of the *Manifesto* were well on their way to becoming part of our state and national laws through the use of patient gradualism — so much so that today few even recognize them for what they are: Marxism.

There is still a great deal of communist influence on the "American" scene that people need to know about and ultimately rectify. The reason is that, as Marx said, certain steps necessitate future actions that will ultimately lead to a totalitarian government if not reversed. We shall give examples as we proceed.

We will not get into an "academic" study. Rather, we will keep it all very simple. Part of the reason that we have advanced into Marxism is because those promoting it do so using very confounding language, rather than keeping it simple enough to be recognized for what it is right off the bat. However, there are many important passages in the *Manifesto* which it is necessary to elaborate on, since they, while subtle, have a very profound effect on American thought today.

The student who reads the *Manifesto* believing it to be simply the rantings of a deranged mind misses the point. The *Manifesto* is based on human nature, which at times can be very debased, and we need to understand this.

It is also a very complex attack on the Ten Commandments, particularly the Tenth in its abbreviated form: Thou shalt not covet.

So let us begin.

Chapter One

The Commission

One must understand that *The Communist Manifesto* was written due to a commission from a secret organization that played a large part in bringing about the 1848-1849 revolutions in Europe, and was to be used during this specific time period for these upheavals. This secret organization was also involved in other revolutions both before and after this time. It was not an organization that wanted to bring about equality or any other utopian idea, but instead it intended to bring about a new order, an order of control over the people in the name of equality. Plus, it was anti-God, particularly anti-Christian. And, the leaders of this organization intended to be the rulers of this new order.

It all started with an organization which was founded in Bavaria, Germany, in 1776. It came to be known as the Illuminati, and it was a very secret sect whose design was to obliterate all religion and consolidate all governments into a single, one-world government to be ruled by them — by the leaders of the Illuminati.

If one were to look at this from a spiritual viewpoint, one could believe that the liberty movement building in 18th-century America based on Christianity necessitated a counter-"revolution," which would become the Illuminati and its offspring, seemingly designed to be an evil imitation of the revolutionary movement in America.

Much has been written about this organization — the Illuminati — and its members. However, a great deal of what has been written is designed not only to obfuscate what the organization stood for and who its leaders were, but — more importantly — to promote the idea that it was dissolved immediately after being exposed. In other words, forget about it, it no longer exists.

The very short story is that the Illuminati continued to exist after being discovered, and established front groups throughout Europe. Their infiltration reached the United States via Americans who studied in select German universities, French agents under the control of the French Revolutionary government, and Americans sympathetic to the French Revolution. This European revolution, it is important to add, was very different from the American Revolution in that, rather than being based on Christianity, it was based on the *elimination* of Christianity, or any religion, with the state being supreme.

The tactic used to hide the influence of the Illuminati was to pretend it had been dissolved, then let it descend into public obscurity, then have it re-emerge under "new" leadership and a new name — at least new *public* leadership.

By and large, the French connection was exposed early on in America, but the German connection proceeded with minimal exposure.

Frederick Engels said that the organization that commissioned him and Marx to write the *Manifesto* was the League of Outlaws, which was "in reality not much more than a German branch of the French secret societies and especially of the *Société des Saisons*" (Society of the Seasons), with goals "the same as those of other Parisian secret societies of the period."

Engels also penned, in an article "On the History of the Communist League":

> In 1836 the most extreme ... elements of the secret democratic-republican Outlaws' League ... split off and formed the new secret League of the Just.... The League was at that time actually not much more than the German branch of the French secret societies....
>
> Originally published Nov. 12-26, 1885 in
> *Sozialdemokrat: Marx and Engels Selected Works*,
> Vol. 3, Progress Publishers, Moscow, 1970

From this League of Outlaws, after it fragmented into the League of the Just, Marx and Engels ultimately manipulated themselves into being the philosophical leaders of the communist conspiracy.

There was a great deal more regarding the secret organization, but we quote only the above to establish the fact that these people deal in secret societies. In addition to an open agenda, they have a secret one that even the rank and file of their organization knows little, if anything, about. Engels also mentioned the names of those who were the harbingers and wellspring of the movement (who were also second-generation Illuminati leaders).*

In America today, no one is allowed to entertain any ideas about a master conspiracy and still be respected by the mass media, the mainstream Republican leaders, or anyone to the left of them.

Yet, it is interesting that nearly every federal case brought against someone includes the charge of conspiracy. Criminals engage in conspiracy, the Mafia engages in conspiracy, the crooked financier engages in conspiracy, even the cheating spouse engages in conspiracy, but we are led to believe that politicians do not (unless, of course, they are conservative

---

* For further information on this influence on the early years in America, we recommend *To the Victor Go the Myths & Monuments* by this author, available at ShopJBS. org.

politicians).

Consider for a moment that almost everything one does is planned, from buying a house to buying groceries after putting together a shopping list. The same is true with industry and business, as any mid-level manager involved with business "strat plans" and product development processes can richly attest. Nothing happens in the economy by businessmen that isn't planned — if it isn't planned, it doesn't get done. Even though planning is an elemental aspect of life, we are supposed to think that it is not so in corrupt politics — we are led to believe results are accidents, or the lack of experience or education on the part of the participants.

Regardless of those involved, planning in secret for an evil purpose is a *conspiracy*.

The general population is not allowed to believe in a political conspiracy even though, historically, the conspiracy's leaders (such as Engels) have admitted there is one. The idea, if it comes up, is that there are no political conspiracies. Don't look behind the curtain, Dorothy.

Over the years there have been many prominent men who have alluded to a conspiracy existing in the body politic, but few have ever heard their statements since they have been systematically purged from the texts studied at all levels of academia.

The list of witnesses is long, but just a few quotes will suffice to demonstrate that there have been those who recognize that a political conspiracy exists.

President Woodrow Wilson wrote:

> Some of the biggest men in the United States, in the field of commerce, and manufacture, are afraid of somebody, are afraid of something. They know that

there is a power somewhere so organized, so subtle, so watchful, so interlocked, so complete, so pervasive, that they had better not speak above their breath when they speak in condemnation of it.

> Woodrow Wilson, *The New Freedom*, New York: Doubleday, Page and Company, 1913, pp.13-14

Winston Churchill and Benjamin Disraeli, both of whom served as prime minister of Great Britain, also referred to this conspiracy.

Disraeli twice mentioned things pertaining to this subject. First he wrote:

> So you see ... the world is governed by very different personages from what is imagined by those who are not behind the scenes.
>
> *Coningsby*, 1844

And later,

> The governments of the present day have to deal not merely with other governments, with emperors, kings, or ministers, but also with secret societies which have everywhere their unscrupulous agents, and can at the last moment upset all the government's plans.
>
> Speech at Aylesbury,
> Great Britain, September 10, 1876

Winston Churchill got closer to the truth of the matter:

> From the Days of Spartacus-Weishaupt (who founded the secret order of the Illuminati on May 1, 1776) to those of Karl Marx ... this world-wide

conspiracy for the overthrow of civilization and for the reconstitution of society on the basis of arrested development, of envious malevolence, and impossible equality, has been steadily growing. It played ... a definitely recognizable part in the tragedy of the French Revolution. It has been the mainspring of every subversive movement during the Nineteenth Century....

"Zionism versus Bolshevism,"
Illustrated Sunday Herald (London),
February 8, 1920

Of course, this would include Marxism.

Any student of political history who ignores the existence of the Illuminati does himself a great disservice. There are many historical and political pundits who dismiss the influence and continuation of this organization, but the existence of the Illuminati is a fact. The debate is over how powerful they were, and when — or if — they dissolved. The truth is that it is a provable fact that they continued on for many years after their obituary was written in "history."

The denial of the Illuminati's influence is certainly a problem in Europe, and it is almost absolute in the United States among Establishment historians.

We include here one last example of the Illuminati's influence, as the reader may have been seeing it before his eyes all along but may not have contemplated the significance of it.

Illuminism has two main goals that have remained consistent over time, and these are key to understanding the conspiracy itself and the ongoing chain of events that has brought us to the present day of worldwide strife and turmoil. These are the elimination of God, and the building of a one-world government, to be run by them. There are many issues that come to bear to achieve these goals, but they all distill down to these two.

One of the key organizations, run by perhaps the most important member of the Illuminati in Revolutionary France, Nicholas Bonneville, was the Cercle Social, or Social Circle. It served as an activist think tank regarding how to subvert any society and promote Illuminism.

Karl Marx and Frederick Engels referred to the Social Circle in their book *The Holy Family*, published in February 1845, three years prior to *The Communist Manifesto*:

> The revolutionary movement which began in 1789 in the Cercle Social ... gave rise to the communist idea ... re-introduced in France after the Revolution of 1830.... This ... is the idea of the new world order.

This is the *communist* idea of a New World Order. This was not a new concept in 1845, but the quote demonstrates that communism came out of the Cercle Social of Revolutionary France led by an Illuminati member, and tells us a great deal about the beginnings of the communist movement and the idea of a New World Order.

Some modern translations of *The Communist Manifesto* use the term new world *system* rather than new world *order* to confuse or mislead readers, since many people who have the same goals as Marx and Engels use the term today. They do not want the reader to recognize that "new world order" is a communist term.

One might mull over in his mind the various world leaders who have used the term New World Order to describe what they want to achieve, such as Fidel Castro and Mikhail Gorbachev, attendees at World Economic Forum meetings, and— regrettably — certain American presidents.

So, we have set the stage for the purpose of *The Communist Manifesto* and the commission by a secret society to write it: to serve as a recruiting tool for the machinations of this secret society, and to allow that organization to influence the people to its advantage and manipulate them into being ruled by a few megalomaniacs in the name of equality, using human nature to appeal to the masses.

Chapter Two
Breaking Down Morality

According to the opening of the *Manifesto* by Marx, the *Manifesto* was to be published in the English, French, German, Italian, Flemish, and Danish languages. This gives us a clue as to the areas targeted for their propaganda, where the primary strengths of the communists lay at the time, and where they hoped they could initiate communist revolutions.

A second-generation organization of the Illuminati, the Carbonari, had its base primarily in Italy but was scattered throughout most of Western Europe and America. The Carbonari and the communists were supposedly rivals, but they cooperated a great deal from 1830 to 1870, both in Europe and the United States.

The *Manifesto* starts off relating a pseudo-history of the development of Western man, which was an attempt to influence the mind of the reader to separate the classes overall into those who rule and those who are ruled: the bourgeoisie and the proletariat. The entire idea was to divide people in order to get them opposing each other in class warfare.

Those who study the lives of Marx and Engels will see that both of them were prejudiced, not just against what they called the bourgeoisie, but against certain races as well. This would have been counterproductive to promote in the *Manifesto*, however, as the intent at the time was to unite enough people to their cause. Although racial hatred would not have helped them build the revolution at that moment in time, it was to become a primary tool to be used by the communists later. Marx, even though he came from a Christian-Jewish family, was antisemitic; Engels hated Slavs and wanted them all exterminated. Both felt the same way about Africans. Communists and other totalitarian socialists went on to conduct repeated campaigns of mass murder and genocide in the bloody decades following the publication of the *Manifesto*.

Then, in Chapter II, Marx goes on to unite the communists with the proletariat, declaring that the communists are the champions of the proletariat workers. In the process, he attacks the concept of the family.

The family has been the basic unit of civilization since the dawn of time or the Garden of Eden, depending on what you believe. Strike a blow to this basic building block of civilized society, and you have the basis for reshaping all of society.

At the same time, the "individual" comes under attack in favor of the class. The destruction of any idea of individualism means that every person comes under the control of the state for the benefit of the state. Of course, this is presented as being best for the common good. When reading the *Manifesto*, one has to understand that, in reality, the term "class" means the state. This is because it is far more acceptable to the reader if he thinks he will be part of a group, rather than controlled by the government under a new name.

Thinking back over history, has the "common good" been responsible for progress, or has it been the free-thinking individual who has supplied the ideas for the progress made, relative to new inventions, systems of government, and societal improvements? Some enterprising individual invented a new product or system, and that invention or idea was promoted by various means into the general population.

Generally speaking, society as a whole tends to stay in the rut it is used to, whether it is the use of tools or behavior. And, many taboos existed, and still exist, around the world as a result of religious or societal influence. In other words, society doesn't invent — individuals do.

When formed into herds, people do not fare well. They must be free to think for themselves if there is to be progress. Moral individualism is what produces progress and liberty.

There will always be people who cannot succeed in providing a decent, or what is considered a decent, living for themselves and/or their family. However, the process of government providing for people has far worse consequences for everyone. History has shown that in the long run, all people suffer under a system that ostensibly provides economic equality for all.

For, in practice, those who rule live very well; the rest of the people, not so much.

At the same time, providing for those who are poor never solves the problem, since government always seems to build a power structure in the name of helping the poor. In America, we have been fighting the so-called War on Poverty for decades, but the number of poor always grows larger — along with the bureaucracy that is intended to eliminate poverty.

If one thinks that the number of poor is decreasing, they haven't been visiting very many of our cities around the country where people are living on the streets. When the War on Poverty started, this was rare.

Some people blame this condition on the drug problem. Here again, though, the War on Drugs has been a failure as well. The only thing the War on Drugs has succeeded in is the effort to build government power to the detriment of constitutionally protected rights. War — any war — is recognized explicitly by communist doctrine as a necessary strategy for building the communist total state.

Thus, the War on Poverty has nothing to do with helping the poor. In fact, the only means by which equality can be established economically is for no one to own anything. More properly defined, this could be called the doctrine of universal impoverishment. The few people not subject to this universal impoverishment would be those running the show. Ultimately, this is the aim of the communists as well as the so-called socialists.

The state will own everything and the people nothing — yet it is all done in the name of the people. The idea is that the government will provide for the needs of the people, supposedly on an equitable basis. Yet, this has never happened in any socialist or communist state.

The rulers of the state will control everything; therefore, they will — and do — live much better. There is no communist or socialist state where the rulers live at the same economic level as the people. The rulers enjoy upscale housing and second-home vacation retreats buried deep in the pristine countryside, kept out of sight of the "normal" people.

Control is more important than ownership — especially if the government regulates all property. In some countries a form of Marxism called *fascism* was developed. The people would not accept full communism at the time in those countries, so an ersatz form was developed.

Fascism is a subset of communism in that it has the same end in mind relative to control by the few at the top. They do not take property away from the people, but they have rules with which they control the people by controlling their property — they tell people where they can live, what type of housing they can build, what they can grow and how much, what they can manufacture and how much, and what the price will be on everything, including wages. The fools still mow "their" grass because the law or zoning requires it.

That is, if the government allows a lawn. Visitors to Europe, for instance, may have noticed that most urban dwellings do not have lawns as we know them in America. Large estates and parks yes, but rarely single-family urban dwellings.

Communism doesn't pretend to allow ownership as does fascism. Under communism the government owns and controls everything outright.

America started out with nearly total freedom, generally moderated only by a common moral standard: you could do anything until it violated the rights of another.

In regard to property, our Founders believed that private property was sacred, and many said so. They understood that ownership of property, free from government control, was essential for a free people.

James Madison, the fourth president of the United States and often referred to as the Father of the Constitution, said:

> Government is instituted to protect property of every sort ... this being the end of government.... That is not a just government, nor is property secure under it, where property which a man has ... is violated by arbitrary seizures of one class of citizens for the services of the rest.

John Adams, our second president, said several things about private property. A couple of quotes indicate his wisdom:

> The moment the idea is admitted into society that property is not as sacred as the laws of God, anarchy and tyranny commence.

And,

> Property is surely a right of mankind as real as liberty.

Adams also stated the reason God is so important to a free people. Although he saw and battled the nascent organization which evolved into communism, Jacobinism, he wasn't talking about socialism at the time:

> Our Constitution was made only for a moral and religious people. It is wholly inadequate to the government of any other.

From this statement we see that the communist goal of eliminating God in America is a direct attack on the Constitution itself.

And this gets into the general but prime reason for the communists' goal of the elimination of God: They do not want anything to be a higher authority than the state. They do not want anything which will contradict the edicts of the state. The state rulers want absolute power by being the absolute authority. And, if one really looks at the full meaning of the Ten Commandments, they find that they forbid socialism in any form, particularly the Tenth Commandment in its abbreviated form: Thou shalt not covet.

The primary trap used by Marx in the *Manifesto* was that under communism all people would be equal in property. In other words, those who could not or did not own property would be living the same as everyone else. At least they believed that it would be better than what they had. It never specifies this in the *Manifesto*, but it is implied. And this hope is based on covetousness.

So we begin to see that communism is in complete opposition to

God's word. One will live in one world or the other. One will obey God, or the state ruled by those who lust for power (or those who will be overcome and ultimately corrupted by power).

For as the axiom Lord Acton coined points out: Power tends to corrupt. And, absolute power corrupts absolutely.

No exceptions.

American Exceptionalism is in direct opposition to communism and the *Manifesto*. Today in American schools, the Marxists have enough control that the basic documents of the Americanist movement either are not taught at all, or are not taught to a level of being *understood*.

The basic document which propelled the liberty movement into open rebellion against the British Crown was the Declaration of Independence.

While the vast number of Americans stare back at the questioner as to where we get our fundamental rights, many conservatives *do* understand that we get our rights from God. When asked how they know this, they will cite the second paragraph of the Declaration of Independence, wherein it states:

> We hold these truths to be self-evident, that all men are created equal, that they are endowed by their Creator with certain unalienable Rights, that among these are Life, Liberty and the pursuit of happiness.

It does not list all our rights, just three, and of those three, only one is a singular one: Life. Yet even this has come to have more than one component as modern debate swirls around abortion and other aspects of life. Our Founders never dreamed that Life would be debated as it is today with abortion and euthanasia. Liberty and the pursuit of happiness span a great deal of human activity, as we shall see, and all of it is based on morality.

However, the first paragraph of the Declaration usually

goes unnoticed, though it is very important to the whole of the Declaration:

> When in the Course of human events, it becomes necessary for one people to dissolve the political bands which have connected them with another, and to assume among the powers of the earth, the separate and equal station to which the Laws of Nature and of Nature's God entitle them, a decent respect to the opinions of mankind requires that they should declare the causes which impel them to the separation.

"The ... equal station to which the Laws of Nature and of Nature's God entitle them...." In these words the Founders stated that God not only places them in an equal position with other governments, *but in essence requires them to take that position and maintain it free from encumbrances.*

By their words they have declared that they are a movement independent of and free from any government which does not follow God's law. They go on within the body of the document to give examples of the violations by the British Crown of the rights of the people, some of which are being done today, or are actively being pursued, by our own government. We have come full circle due to the Marxist incursion into our body politic.

To quote John Adams again:

> Our Constitution was made only for a moral and religious people. It is wholly inadequate to the government of any other.

In other words, freedom is only possible under God's law, and without this basis, there is no freedom. Without this moral basis you will have a government that controls everything, eventually.

In a letter to H. Niles in 1818, Adams wrote:

> The Revolution was in the minds and hearts of the people; a change in their religious sentiments, of their duties and obligations.... This radical change in the principles, opinion, sentiments, and affections of the people was the real American Revolution.

Note that Adams states that it was a *change* — the people did not start out that way. The marvelous country we have demonstrates that society can change for the better. Lately, Marxist forces have been doing the opposite: removing society from a moral basis, reflected in the rise of public disorder, crime, government corruption, etc. More importantly, there is a lack of assuming responsibility overall, by both individuals and communities. People must work to make things more moral overall in our country to save it from Marxism.

The problem with the latter is that too many people do not know what is right, or are unwilling to assume the responsibility to do what is right, either in the sense of working to return our country to basic principles or being willing to assume the responsibility to live free from government benefits. These benefits can be in the form of either money or personal advantages in regulations over other aspects of the economy, business, or individuals.

Government benefits always come with a price, and that price in the long run is totalitarianism. Not necessarily at first, but eventually, as certain steps at the beginning result in government controls in the end.

For, as already mentioned, with benefits comes bureaucracy, and with bureaucracy come regulations, and fines, and often prison if the regulations are not followed. And, taxes to supply the benefits. The taxes are always more than the benefits bestowed, since it takes a great deal of money to sustain a bureaucracy to hand out the benefits and regulate their use.

Many people are becoming aware of the changes that have been taking place in our schools over the years, since they have been accelerating recently. However, these changes have been going on for many decades, slowly, using patient gradualism so as not to alarm parents.

We shall discuss what is behind what has been happening in the schools further into this volume, but for now it is sufficient to state that banning the mention in the public schools of God or the foundation of God in our government is leading us away from the basic fundamentals of Americanism. This is showing up more and more in the general behavior of our youth.

Our system was based on the self-governing of the people, since they were basically a moral people. Once morality breaks down, liberty breaks down and people have to be restrained from violating others' rights. But the restraints are placed on everyone, not just the lawbreakers. One striking example is the ownership of guns.

The lawlessness we see currently in various sections and cities of the country is a direct reflection of the lack of teaching the children morality and responsibility — in the homes as well as in the schools. And, sadly, there is this same lack of teaching even in churches, some of which preach civil disobedience against moral authority.

The elimination of the Ten Commandments from the schools and public buildings is a direct reflection of the Marxist attack on American society. We shall explore the meaning and significance of this further on.

Chapter Three
The *Manifesto* Means to Build Communist Government

Marx refers to the fact that, in spite of changes over time, the basic foundations of civilization have survived. Thus, these foundations — God, family, and country — must be eliminated.

He calls for the elimination of private property as the key to the rupture with traditional ideas, and we shall discuss this later.

However, one aspect of government rises as more important to Marx:

> We have seen … that the first step in the revolution
> by the working class is to raise the proletariat to the
> position of ruling class, to win the battle of democracy.

Embodied in this quote is a very important aspect of communism, and an illustration of just how much influence the Marxists have had on the American psyche.

First, let us point out that the idea of *equality* professed by the Marxists is a lie, for in this quote Marx says that they want "to raise the proletariat to the position of *ruling class*." So much for equality. Trading one ruling class for another is not equality.

This is pure and simple pandering to those out of power to replace one power structure with another — the implication being that those who are at the bottom of the scale will rise to rule those currently at the top.

But the most important point we wish to make here is that Marx wants to have a *democracy*. Now, many people who read the *Manifesto* see this passage and think that Marx is lying, that he throws this in there to cater to people with the idea that all will be able to decide their own future at the polls.

Voting for one's representatives is a lot different than having a democracy. Let us start off by saying that our Founders gave us a *republic*, not a democracy. You can find no Founder who supported a democracy at the time the Constitution was written. Quite the opposite. For instance, John Adams, in a letter to John Taylor in 1814, said this:

> Democracy never lasts long. It soon wastes, exhausts and murders itself. There never was a democracy yet, that did not commit suicide.

As to whether we are a republic or a democracy, when we stand and pledge allegiance to the flag, we pledge "to the *Republic* for which it stands" — not the *democracy*.

Marx and Engels understood that democracy is an unstable system of government that can be used to transition into communism.

Relatively recently, Jan Kozak, a high-ranking member of the Czechoslovakian Communist Party after World War II, gave a speech before a conclave of loyal party members wherein he delineated how the communists had taken power in Czechoslovakia. He divided his talk into major sections, with subtitles such as "From Capitalism to Socialism Through Democracy," and "From Democracy, to Socialism, to Marxism."

He explained how this was achieved, affirming that the road to communism travels through democracy first.*

We are a republic. You will not find the word democracy in the federal Constitution or in any of the 50 state constitutions. What you will find in the federal Constitution is that it mandates that every state shall have a republican form of government — a republic.

> ARTICLE IV, SECTION 4. The United States shall guarantee to every State in this Union a republican form of government....

In other words, a republic.

If the American people do not even know what form of government we have and instead believe that we are a democracy, then we are being set up for a transition from what we have, through a democracy, into Marxism.

Benjamin Franklin understood how precarious even a stable form of government can be, and how easily a republic can be lost if the people are not aware of the dangers of doing so. In his reply to a lady who asked him outside of the convention hall in Philadelphia about what form of government they had formulated, he replied, "A republic, Ma'am, if you can keep it."

If you can keep it.

Democracies always turn the majority against the minority. In the long run, there is no protection for minorities in a democracy — from excessive taxation, property confiscation, or even death. World history contains one example after another of majorities eliminating the minorities whenever governments are not bound down with the chains of an inviolate constitution.

---

* This speech was reprinted in the West under the title *And Not a Shot Is Fired*, available from ShopJBS.org.

21

The entire Middle East is an example of Muslims eliminating minority sects of other Muslims — as well as Christians and Jews.

The *Manifesto* goes on to delineate the steps necessary to change a country into a communist state. Marx states that the measures outlined will be different in different countries. This is especially true for the United States. Since we are so very different from other countries, more steps than the ten must be utilized to change our system into a communist one. Of course, the first major step is to change us into a democracy.

As Marx says:

Nevertheless, in the most advanced countries the following will be pretty generally applicable:

1. Abolition of property in land and application of all rents of land to public purposes.
2. A heavy progressive or graduated income tax.
3. Abolition of all right of inheritance.
4. Confiscation of the property of all emigrants and rebels.
5. Centralization of credit in the hands of the State, by means of a national bank with State capital and an exclusive monopoly.
6. Centralization of the means of communication and transport in the hands of the State.
7. Extension of factories and instruments of production owned by the State, the bringing into cultivation of waste lands, and the improvement of the soil generally in accordance with a common plan.
8. Equal liability of all to labor. Establishment of industrial armies, especially for agriculture.
9. Combination of agriculture with manufacturing

industries; gradual abolition of the distinction between town and country by a more equable distribution of population over the country.
10. Free education for all children in public schools. Abolition of children's factory labor in its present form. Combination of education with industrial production, etc., etc.

These ten steps still constitute the core of the changes necessary in most countries, although over time a few of them have been adjusted somewhat as a result of modern changes and inventions.

Step 1 — Abolition of Property: The abolition of private property remains the hallmark of communism. We have departed considerably from the private property rights our forefathers protected for us. We can demonstrate this by asking and answering two questions.

If you rent and do not pay your rent, what happens to you? Answer: You are evicted.

If you own your property outright and do not pay your taxes, what happens to you? Answer: You are evicted.

What is the difference?

You can call taxes either rent or payments on your property which never cease. You can call yourself a property owner, but the government will tax you year after year, forever, and it will regulate what you can do with that property. You consider yourself an owner, but you are regulated and taxed on it until you die — then someone else gets to pay the taxes and be regulated by the government.

In case you haven't recognized it yet, this is not liberty. It is a form of Marxism. However, most people have grown so used to it that they don't even notice, or if they do, they feel it is normal.

Step 2 — Progressive Income Tax: Well, we did that at the turn of the 20th century. *The Communist Manifesto* had been in print and widely read for over a half a century, but the American people fell for the Marxist initiative for a graduated income tax nonetheless.

Step 3 — Abolition of Inheritance: While not eliminating all rights of inheritance, the federal government, along with many state governments, confiscates certain amounts, or percentages, of what people inherit. These amounts vary over time depending on the incumbent political party. In some cases, it has meant that the heirs must sell out to pay the taxes, since they are in the condition known as "land poor." The land is worth more than any income or cash on hand the heirs may have, and its intrinsic worth is taxed, not the liquidity. Some states tax the estate at the federal level, making it a double tax.

Step 4 — Confiscation of Property of Rebels: There is only one time that this has been done by the federal government, and that was during the Civil War and to a certain degree during the Reconstruction Period which immediately followed the war.

Step 5 — National Bank: This is, for all practical purposes, the Federal Reserve System. It was set up by bankers to serve *certain bankers* as a consortium. The best book to read about this is the bestseller *The Creature From Jekyll Island*, by G. Edward Griffin.*

Since the founding of the "Fed," the government has used the resulting system of fiat money inflation — essentially reducing the value of money year over year — to steal vast quantities of wealth from Americans. As a result, the value of American currency has been reduced by 99 percent. The stunning

---

* Available from ShopJBS.org.

consequence of this deliberate theft of American prosperity is seen in dramatic increases in prices — which in fact result from a dollar being worth far less today than when the Fed was created. Commodities which cost a dollar in 1914 now cost one hundred dollars. Certain items have had their costs held at a lower loss by the invention of new techniques of growing or manufacturing.

For an easy illustration of the scale of inflation since the founding of the Fed, one can check mail order catalogs from that period against retail prices today. In 1916, for example, major mail-order retailer Montgomery Ward offered white, high-top "tennis gym and camp" shoes for $0.95. This was the most expensive shoe in that category, appearing on page 241 of that particular catalog. In brown, men's low-top shoes in that category were as low as $0.53. Today, men's athletic shoes can range in price from $50 to $100 — or even much more. In spring 2024, for example, Amazon sold the modern equivalent of the Montgomery Ward white high-top in the form of the Adidas Men's Web Boost Running shoe for $120.49 in men's size 12.5.

The change in the value of money is the result of deliberate policy, not the result of some dim, mystical process whereby the money changes over time.

The Fed was sold to the people as the answer to problems with bank failures and the loss of wealth by many people which had occurred in the years after the Civil War and in the early 1900s. Instead, though, it built a giant conglomeration which served the government and robbed everyone of their wealth. Again, read *The Creature From Jekyll Island.*

Step 6 — Centralization of Communication and Transport: While we have the Bill of Rights, which protects our freedom of speech and press, since its writing, all new means of communication have come under the control of the federal government, as outlined by Marx. The telegraph, telephone, radio, television, internet, etc. — all must be licensed by the government. And, the regulations pertaining to each one vary. Moreover, these regulations can be and have been used to prevent freedom of speech.

These means of communication are today heavily censored in conjunction with the state, particularly our intelligence community. Those who are connected with "alternative" types of broadcasting are aware of this problem, and most Americans believe that what constitutes the mass media today deserves to be called Fake News.

Transportation is likewise heavily controlled through the process of licensing, manufacturing requirements, speed limits, use of the rail system, etc. The environmental movement, which is essentially Marxist, wants total control over the use of private transportation, such as by replacing cars with so-called public transportation. The movement to implement "15-minute cities" is, in fact, an effort to eliminate the average person's ability to travel.

Step 7 — State Ownership of Production: This has evolved into the control of all land through the use of environmental regulations under the leadership of the United Nations, through such programs as Agenda 21, Agenda 2030, and the Great Reset. Pick your title; they are all the same thing, emanating from the same source.

Control is accomplished initially using local governments belonging to UN organizations such as the International Council for Local Environmental Initiatives (ICLEI). Furthermore, treaties by the federal government in so-called free trade agreements have begun the process of land and manufacturing controls. (To hide the UN connection, ICLEI changed its name to "ICLEI – Local Governments for Sustainability," since too many people were waking up to the fact that an international agency was controlling their local government.)

Step 8 — All Must Labor: We have not yet started to require all to labor, although there are many Republican initiatives that require people to work to be able to collect government handouts. This can only lead to one conclusion: The solution is no federal handouts. Whatever charity is necessary should be accomplished locally, through individual initiative, charitable organizations, and churches. Local people know their neighbors and situation better, and charity is usually done best on a volunteer basis, easing taxation on the poor who are not partakers of the handouts.

Step 9 — State Distribution of Land: The distribution of people over the land has changed over the years, and now the Marxists want all to live in centralized apartment complexes, so they can better control the surveillance and movement of the people. More and more cities have huge apartment complexes. Once the ideal was to move into suburbia, to own a home and a piece of land you could call your own: private property. Efforts are underway in many states to remove local ordinances that make it difficult to build massive multi-unit complexes and transfer control to state-level agencies, with the goal of ending individual property ownership. As with most communist efforts, the rallying cry is one of envy — the rich have houses and the poor can't afford housing, so we must forcibly switch to mega complexes of "affordable" apartments. One might be tempted to call these "communes," but that terminology went out with the Soviet Union.

Step 10 — Government Control of Education: The Marxists do not want any children homeschooled or educated in private schools. Most of the Founders of the United States were homeschooled to some degree, even some presidents. All of them who had any formal schooling attended private institutions. If the state rules the schools, then what the state wants taught will be what the students learn. The highest percentage of public-school attendance occurred several decades ago. With the deterioration of the results of government schooling, parents are increasingly looking to alternatives for their children.

In some major cities, such as Baltimore, it is very hard to find graduating seniors who can read or do math. This is an outcome common in many of our large metropolitan areas.

This author has talked to many young people who do not have enough grasp of the basics of American history to even understand what one is talking about. By young, we mean 30 years and under.

For example, we wrote a book with the title *Benedict Biden*. Far too many young adults do not even get the implication of the title, since they do not even know who Benedict Arnold was — the first major traitor of the American Revolution. The story of Arnold used to be universally taught in the schools to help students understand that the lack of morality can lead to treason. But, that was in an earlier America.

State-operated schools teach state-approved curricula. Plus, the teachers unions are socialist at best, belonging to an international union run by socialists and communists called Education International. It was started by an American who was a leader in the Socialist Party of America, Albert Shanker. He was also an advisor to the Young People's Socialist League. If you spend enough time on the internet, you can prove this for yourself.

Not all teachers are socialists. It is just that the teachers unions and their aligned bureaucrat enablers, using the power of government, have taken over the schools — as well as the teachers who do not like the unions. This author has seen more than a few classrooms where communist leaders have been lauded and Marxism has been openly taught. Indeed, little attempt is made to hide this these days.

One of the problems with homeschooling, which is just now becoming apparent, is that the parents did not receive a basic education in their schools, and therefore they now have difficulty teaching the fundamentals to their own children.

Believe it or not, parents in many homeschool situations are now learning right along with their own children.

Many say that people no longer read — this is due to the fact that too many cannot read.

Chapter Four
Baloney

After delineating the ten primary steps for communizing a country, Marx goes on to deliver some of the most ridiculous paragraphs in the entire *Manifesto*:

> When, in the course of development, class distinctions have disappeared, and all production has been concentrated in the hands of a vast association of the whole nation, the public power will lose its political character....

And,

> In place of the old bourgeois society, with its classes and class antagonisms, we shall have an association, in which the free development of each is the condition for the free development of all.

Anyone who has been involved in a free association of people knows full well that no association is completely harmonious. This will vary from group to group; however, people, since they are individuals, have different opinions of who should lead an organization, what the direction of the organization should be, and even what the wording should be of what may be published concerning the unanimous opinion of the association members.

For people to be free, they must have different opinions

about everything, so if the communist-led association referred to by Marx is truly free, it can never, ever, be "harmonious" without coercion. We're talking about coercion either imposed from within by those who really control the association by their out-organizing the mass of members within, or imposed from above by a stratum of enforcers, such as from some layer of government.

Free people are never in total agreement.

So, Marx must have had something else in mind. We now know this was the superior organization of the communists led by a secret society, as Engels told us: a behind-the-scenes organization which had goals unknown to the "rabble" they ruled.

Of course, by the future projection of time of this reference by Marx, this cabal would have already been in control, and the secret members of the communist movement would have already been established in positions of power over the "association." Again, the "association" includes *all* of the people.

And, what do you think might happen to people who find themselves at odds, however slightly, with the "association"? We don't have to guess at the answer, as history is full of examples — even if that history is largely ignored or placed in the "memory hole" by communists and their fellow travelers in the media and academia.

In fact, we have seen that in communism, those who disagree with the aims of the "association" are eliminated — in some cases by the millions. This was certainly true in Russia and China by many tens of millions. Those two communist nations, individually and combined, conducted mass murder in the 20th century on a scale that can scarcely be imagined.

So, based on the actual experience of communist rule in a free association which exists in harmony, Marx's vision is not of utopia, but Hell.

Those who think through the words of Marx know that what he talks about in the *Manifesto* is what is commonly referred to today as a pipe dream. But, those who do not think through them fall for the Marxist "pie in the sky" (another modern saying).

When considering what Marx says, it is necessary to compare his writing to the way he actually lived his life. He neglected his family, and never had what one would call a real job. His success was in telling people what to think, while he himself was what most would call a failure. He did have some income from his writing for such publications as the *New-York Tribune*, but this was not a steady income, as it amounted to around 500 articles in 11 years.

He was a successful schemer for leadership over the secret organization behind the communist movement, but this was done with a great deal of help from his collaborator Engels.

One could call Marx a success in writing to build the communist movement, but the results have been disastrous for the people of the Earth, from the first communist revolutions to today.

For instance, China is not a utopia for individualism or true freedom, and the same can be said for Vietnam, North Korea, Cuba, etc.

This is true for all countries with a communist government, even those which pretend to not have one today, such as Russia, Belarus, Ukraine, the various "stans," et al.

Regarding the current conflict between Russia and Ukraine, it is not the first time that totalitarian countries have been at war with one another. Recall that Hitler and Stalin warred with each other. Bear in mind, again, that war is a tool deliberately used to move toward communist goals. Look carefully, then, at those who are most rabidly in favor of war or who start wars.

War, or conflict, has always been — and will always be — used to manipulate the people, either internally or externally, by their own government, to move them in the direction the powers-that-be desire. Sometimes it is used simply to solidify support for the government in the name of the war effort.

In the case of communism, there is always conflict — either real or imagined — created by the government to keep the people in check and focused on some enemy — either real or imagined — and to keep them worried about something other than their own oppressive government.

Conflict is also used by government, when it has enough power, to keep voters focused on imaginary dangers from its opponents. A recent example is the Biden administration's attempt to demonize any opponents who tended to be more constitutionalist in their quest for better government, even referring to them as Nazis or terrorists when the opposite was the truth.

Another basic technique coming out of Marxism is class warfare, although it has been harder to utilize in America since the average "Joe" can get ahead if he really wants to. The opportunities of freedom as we know it allow anyone to succeed — if he really wants to work for success and not have it handed to him on a silver platter.

All of this Marxist ideology is baloney. But, the worst part of the *Manifesto* is the idea of the elimination of private property as the basis for freedom. This is the height of baloney, which we shall look at in the next chapter.

Chapter Five

Private Property

It is clear that the *Manifesto* was written primarily for Europeans by the statistics Marx uses to illustrate the problem with private property:

> You are horrified at our intending to do away with private property. But in your existing society, private property is already done away with for nine-tenths of the population; its existence for the few is solely due to its non-existence in the hands of those nine-tenths. You reproach us, therefore, with intending to do away with a form of property, the necessary condition for whose existence is the non-existence of any property for the immense majority of society.

And, this was the condition in Europe.

However, in America it was the opposite — the majority of the people *could* enjoy the ownership of private property. Indeed, the very idea of owning private property served as a basis for liberty as we know it.

The Founders of the United States understood the importance of private property, and built our system based on it. Marxists today do all they can to erode this basis among Americans by making it increasingly difficult for people to own property through all manner of regulations, often through environmental regulations in the name of saving planet Earth.

As a result of this, as well as of economic conditions, more and more people are gravitating toward apartment living, resulting in large apartment complexes in the cities.

We quoted some of the ideas of our Founders concerning private property in Chapter Two.

But, what is property? The *Manifesto* makes it sound as if it is only landed property Marx is concerned about, yet property entails much more than land.

Property is everything necessary for the survival of man in the broadest sense — not only for his survival, but for his pleasure as well.

The Judeo-Christian view is that God put everything on Earth for the benefit of man. Therefore, everything is man's property, under the authority of God, in other words. (Everything, that is, except for other people.)

With this comes the responsibility to husband the land, animals, etc.

America was founded on this Judeo-Christian view. It guaranteed nearly total freedom to the people. It used to be said that a man's home was his castle. This saying came about because no one had the right to invade his home, not even the government. A moat was built around that idea with the Bill of Rights, and it was a pillar of thinking when it came to private property.

Everyone had the right to do with his property as he saw fit as long as he did not violate the rights of others in the process.

Due to the Marxist idea of government, though, the citizens of the United States have come a long way from being able to do with their property whatever they see fit to do. As the size of government has grown over the last two centuries, so have the rules and regulations over private property by all levels of government.

We have already discussed the idea that you do not really "own" your property if the government taxes it, can take it away for non-payment of taxes, and regulates your use of it. Government often goes to the extreme of even making property worthless to the land owner, since increasing regulations may prohibit the use of the land for which it was originally purchased.

An example of this is the government not allowing cattle on land near a river which they claim would become contaminated by the cattle. Taking this even further, now the governments in Europe are attempting to eliminate cows entirely in the name of saving the environment. In mining, minerals and other ores often lay dormant because the government doesn't want the land disturbed. The "protection" of so-called wetlands, sometimes little more than seasonal puddles, is used to prevent the planting of crops. Similar examples, sadly, have become very common.

While you "own" your property, it is regulated by government at all levels as to what you may or may not do with it, through zoning, compacts, environmental regulations, etc. In other words, government controls your property.

These controls may rest lightly on the property owner if he doesn't have any plans for the property which would violate some regulation — which is the case with most homeowners. However, the majority of regulations tend to stifle progress and the economy.

This last statement may seem untrue, but that is because it sometimes is not clear what could have been had the regulations not existed in the first place.

Control is more important than ownership. If you "own" property but government regulations prevent you from using it as you see fit, then you really don't have ownership in the fullest sense of the word.

Gradually, what has been happening in America is the

tightening of the noose of government control over private property and enterprise. In the end, this leads to communism.

If Marx truly were a lover of freedom, he would have advocated the expansion of private property in Europe rather than the confiscation of all private property in land. Protection of natural rights, including the right to private property, has been proven conclusively to lead to dramatic improvements in wealth for all levels of society. If Marx and his followers were really interested in the well-being of the working class, they would not have advocated for the destruction of the right to private property. But, of course, they had the opposite in mind.

It should be noted that "property" entails more than landed property. It includes one's time, labor — even thoughts. Invention comes from one's ability to think "outside of the box," to think freely. In countries where people can think freely, the economy flourishes and the citizens are better off.

Totalitarian states do not progress well. Innovation evaporates because there is no incentive to innovate. Production stagnates because there is no positive incentive to produce. What production does happen does not align with needs, because in the absence of private property ownership and free individual initiative, there is no way for producers to judge need and demand. Again, if this seems doubtful, history offers plentiful examples in the form of the communist totalitarian states of the 20th century: Soviet Russia and Communist China.

In a free society, entrepreneurs take risks because of the potential for reward. If an entrepreneur fails, that failure only causes problems within the circle of influence of the entrepreneur. However, when government is involved, a mistake can affect the entire country.

We like to use the example of Nazi Germany and its vaunted weapons of war that reached the battlefield much too late, or were misused, due to bureaucratic interference. The most famous example was the Messerschmitt Me 262 jet fighter plane, which was kept from use against the British and American bombers over Germany because at first Hitler wanted an anti-tank plane rather than a fighter. This caused a delay in making it a pursuit fighter which would have swept the skies of our bombers before the American Mustang fighters came on the scene.

As a result, in this case, the bureaucratic red tape helped the cause of freedom by helping defeat the German war machine. There are several other examples of adverse bureaucratic interference which could be cited relative to the World War II German war machine.

This author has copies of magazines issued by the Soviet government prior to World War II for distribution around the Western world to convince the reader that Russia was a paradise. It showed smiling faces, workers in the fields, industrial factories, etc., all intended to portray an image of something that did not exist and was a lie. Had Russia not been supplied with the means to win by Britain and the United States, they would have been defeated by Germany. The war materials given to them are staggering in number.

Russia is the largest country in the world, blessed with fine agricultural land and natural riches beyond the wildest dreams of most Western Europeans. Yet under communism it was a basket case.

We could supply several examples of how communist governments have defeated themselves due to too much government, and especially the fear of reporting the lack of efficiency to superiors to give them a true picture of what capabilities they possessed. In a communist state, no one wants to report failure to a superior, since it could lead to dire consequences for the messenger.

One needs accurate data to make major decisions.

But we wander.

The point is, ownership free from government regulation produces progress. It is the other way around when government is all powerful; then civilization regresses. The few at the top do very well; the rest, not so much.

In order to serve the secret cabal behind communism, and for their benefit, Marx sold an idea that was and remains harmful to the people, not for the benefit of the people.

There are those who claim that communism isn't bad, it is just that bad people have tried to implement it.

It should be a clue that *it is always* bad people who try to implement it.

It doesn't work as professed. It only works for megalomaniacs who want power.

Widespread ownership of property works for liberty. The curtailment of private property works for totalitarianism.

The elimination of private property goes against the word of God. What word is that, you say? Try the *Ten Commandments*.

The Fifth Commandment: Thou shalt not steal. Obviously, stealing entails taking property away from another who owns it.

The Eighth Commandment: Thou shalt not bear false witness against thy neighbor. This implies an aspect of property not always noticed — that is lying to rob someone of some level of their freedom and/or property.

The Tenth Commandment gets right down to it: *Thou shalt not covet thy neighbor's house, nor his wife, nor his manservant, nor his ox, nor his ass, nor anything that is thy neighbor's*. This is the essence of private property, and this is more often than not misquoted — or even dropped — when the Ten Commandments are listed today, since it is a complete rejection of socialism.

Keep in mind, these are *commandments*, not suggestions.

These commandments do not pertain only to individuals; they pertain to any grouping of individuals, even one calling itself a government.

The entire platform of socialism/communism is based on the violation of the Tenth Commandment: coveting someone else's property, trying to make everyone equal in property. This is the siren song of Marxism. In reality, the Marxist result is that *no one* has property. That is the only way all can be *equal*.

That is, again, except those in power, who seem to be more equal than others.

In order to establish socialism, two things have to give way: a belief in God, and the idea of people as individuals — thus the modern campaign by Marxists against religion, the elimination of the Ten Commandments from public buildings and schools, and the neglect of our founding documents in the schools.

We say here *socialism* simply because it is part of Marxism leading to complete communism.

Let us again delineate what property includes: It is not simply land as mentioned in the *Manifesto*, but buildings on the land, the fruits of the land, planted grains, animals, etc. It includes inventory and machinery — literally everything that makes up the life of human beings.

Marx concentrates on landed property. However, you can see by the above that if the land belongs to the state, then everything that exists on the land does so as well; Marx just "forgets" to tell the reader that. So one can say that only landed property will be owned by the state, but the hidden aspect of it means everything solid on the land will be owned by the state as well.

It is perhaps worth the time here to remind the reader of the recent slogan championed by the communists of the World Economic Forum, to wit, "you will own nothing and be happy." This is the siren song of communism.

Now, in the name of the environment, even the weather that affects the land comes under the control of the government. They may not actually control the weather, but they are trying to convince the people that by controlling the land they can do so.

Our government was to be a limited one, only strong enough to provide for the protection of the people from invasion and to protect the rights of the people and property. Nowhere in the Constitution does it provide for the people other than the protection of their rights.

Today, the federal government does not even protect us from invasion. What else can you call the mass migration into our country?

Even as the Constitution obviously limited the rule of government, many of the people did not trust the government until a Bill of Rights was added to the Constitution as promised. This spelled out even more restrictions on the government, and with more specificity, stating that the government could pass no laws affecting the freedom of religion, speech, press, etc.

The Bill of Rights even mentioned property.

The Fourth Amendment states, "The right of the people to be secure in their person, houses, papers, and effects, against unreasonable searches and seizures, shall not be violated...."

The Fifth Amendment states that a person cannot "be deprived of life, liberty, or property, without due process of law; nor shall private property be taken for public use without just compensation."

So, one can see immediately that the founding of the United States was in direct opposition to what became the Marxist movement.

The people understood their rights, property and otherwise, and wanted to make sure that they were proclaimed and protected in the Constitution.

Over time, many of these rights have been violated, often with the vast majority of the people either not realizing it due to ignorance, or supporting it due to Marxist campaigns pressuring them to do so.

And, this has been done slowly, patiently, so that the American people would not get excited enough over any one thing to organize to stop it.

Chapter Six

The Death of the Individual, Marriage, and Patriotism

Over and over again, Marx in the *Manifesto* proclaims a desire for the death of the individual, and writes as if the reader should share that desire.

Not just the desire for the demise of the individual, but for the death of the family as well.

As to the latter, he caters to the basest of people: those who wish to divest themselves of family responsibility, for this comes close to what Marx did his entire life when it came to taking care of his own family.

From the *Manifesto*:

> From the moment when labor can no longer be converted into capital, money, or rent, into a social power capable of being monopolized, i.e., from the moment when individual property can no longer be transformed into bourgeois property, into capital, from that moment, you say, individuality vanishes.

Here you begin to see that Marx was not simply talking about landed property alone.

He continues by talking about bourgeois laziness, but the point here is that he is talking about all property, not just farmland, factories, or houses.

Then he proclaims that the family is based on capital:

> Abolition of the family! Even the most radical flare up at this infamous proposal of the Communists.

And,

> On what foundation is the present family, the bourgeois family, based? On capital, on private gain. In its completely developed form this family exists only among the bourgeoisie. But this state of things finds its complement in the practical absence of the family among the proletarians, and in public prostitution.

Marx tries to convince the reader that the middle class, the bourgeoisie, are hedonistic and lacking in morals:

> Our bourgeois, not content with having wives and daughters of their proletarians at their disposal, not to speak of common prostitutes, take the greatest pleasure in seducing each other's wives.

If Marx really believes this, then he must travel in some rather low-life circles, because this was not the norm then, nor is it now. He goes on:

> Bourgeois marriage is in reality a system of wives in common, and thus, at the most, what the communists might possibly be reproached with is that they desire to introduce, in substitution for a hypocritically concealed,

> an openly legalized community of women. For the rest,
> it is self-evident that the abolition of the present system
> of production must bring with it the abolition of the
> community of women springing from that system, *i.e.*,
> of prostitution both public and private.

Again, if he really believes this stuff, his circle of friends and acquaintances must be very narrow and decadent. For this is no more true than, to use an old expression, the man in the moon.

The point is that Marxism does not believe in normal marriage and the family. And, as we have already expressed, Marx lived in a manner which displayed his feelings about his wife and family, which he neglected. In one notorious incident, for example, Marx's wife, Jenny, was away trying to gin up financial support for her struggling family. She was pregnant. Back home, Karl had an affair with the family housekeeper, leading to both his wife and his mistress being pregnant at the same time. His ill-founded complaints about the wealthy were thus merely a reflection of the hatred and disgust he should have felt about his own revolting behavior.

As to patriotism and love of country, the *Manifesto* says:

> The Communists are further reproached with desiring
> to abolish countries and nationalities.
>> The working men have no country. We cannot
> take away from them what they have not got.

Further,

> National differences, and antagonisms between
> peoples, are daily more and more vanishing, owing
> to the development of the bourgeoisie, to freedom

> of commerce, to the world market, to uniformity in
> the mode of production and in the conditions of life
> corresponding thereto.
>
> The supremacy of the proletariat will cause them
> to vanish still faster. United action, of the leading
> civilized countries at least, is one of the first conditions
> for the emancipation of the proletariat.

These passages reveal a great deal about the strategy of the communists for forming their New World Order. First of all, they do not want to support any patriotic ideas, love of country, or separation of countries. They want a one-world government ruled by the proletariat — which actually means the communist organization, with the leaders of the secret cabal as rulers.

Another quote of Marx as it pertains to the above passages, which he made in a speech in Brussels, Belgium, on January 9, 1848, makes the *Manifesto's* remarks more clear:

> (Free trade) breaks up old nationalities.... In a word,
> the free trade system hastens the social revolution.

He would have been even more open if he had said that free trade hastens the New World Order. For you see, the so-called freedom of commerce, world market, uniformity in the mode of production, etc., mentioned in the above quote from the *Manifesto* alludes to what has become the modern scheme of free trade.

Free trade is not free. Once government becomes involved in trade it becomes regulated trade, no matter what the title on the agreement says. Anyone reading the free trade agreements immediately sees that they do three primary things: One, they bring trade under the control of the United Nations; the provisions in the treaties or agreements state as much. Two, the countries involved form a super-governmental committee to regulate and determine the future of not only trade, but banking, manufacturing, and more in the countries involved. And three, they break down the rule of the Constitution in the United States.

The Constitution states that Congress shall regulate trade, yet so-called free trade agreements give that responsibility to other supranational organizations. Free trade agreements are literally unconstitutional if they take the power to regulate trade out of the hands of Congress, but you never hear this coming from even the most die-hard conservative Republican in Congress.

As to the idea of building the communist one-world government, we only have to point to the United States-Mexico-Canada Agreement (USMCA), an agreement highly touted by Republicans. Such New World Order-supporting organizations as the Council on Foreign Relations threw their weight behind the passage of this agreement. Even more revealing as to the end goal of the USMCA were the words of Christian Whiton, who posted an article on Fox News online on October 2, 2018, stating:

> To paraphrase Winston Churchill, this isn't the beginning of the end, but it may be the end of the beginning of creating a ***new world order*** of trade. [Emphasis added.]

At the signing ceremony of the USMCA where the leaders of the three countries spoke, Donald Trump talked about trade while Mexican President Enrique Peña Nieto had a more revealing speech. His comments included such statements as:

> The negotiation of the Mexico-United States-Canada Treaty made it possible to reaffirm the importance of

the ***economic integration*** of North America.

The renegotiation of the new trade agreement sought to safeguard the vision of an ***integrated*** North America. [Emphasis added.]

And,

The Mexican-United States-and-Canada Treaty gives a renewed face toward our ***integration***. [Emphasis added.]

Subsequently, Mexico elected a new president, the openly Marxist Andrés Manuel López Obrador, who met with President Biden to discuss the *political* integration of the three countries based on the USMCA. Every Mexican president since Vicente Fox has advocated merging North America into a single country.

The point is, Marx understood that one of the means by which the world could be united into the New World Order was through so-called free trade agreements. In this manner conservatives could think that they are supporting something good for their country, free trade, but the agreements would lock the countries into an international consortium, which is today the United Nations.

There never has been a non-Marxist as the president of the General Assembly of the UN, and more chairs of the major committees and subcommittees are occupied by Communist China than any other country. This is without taking into account communists from other countries in positions of leadership and responsibility in the UN.

A book could be written about the problems of America's membership in the UN and how the UN is gradually taking over our foreign policy, as well as our internal affairs relative to land, water, air, and many other regulations. Actually, several books have been written about that.*

Marx foresaw the effectiveness of marching toward the New World Order by treaty, both political and economic. Several attempts were made by socialists in Europe and America to form organizations which had the specific goal of a one-world government, ostensibly to stop future wars. However, there never was an initiative to do so on the part of multiple governments until after World War I.

The first major step toward this goal was the League of Nations, which the American people rejected and the U.S. Senate refused to join.

The next major step was the formation of the United Nations. The second half of World War II was used to prepare the minds of the American people for this step. In fact, the idea of the UN's existence was formed in the American mind before the end of hostilities, as noted in many official propaganda pieces in the mainstream media that regularly referred to the efforts of the Allies as the work of the "United Nations."

One such example, of many, appeared on page 30 of *Life* magazine for June 5, 1944. Remarking on a then-recent speech given by Winston Churchill to the British Parliament about foreign relations among allied nations, *Life's* editorial writer remarked: "By chasing 'ideology' out of the United Nations cause, Mr. Churchill did not dispel the world's ideological confusion." The editorialist's intention was to promote the progressivism of then-Senator Robert M. La Follette against what he viewed as the amoral internationalism of Churchill. But that is neither here nor there in the present context. More important is the fact that *Life's* writer referred to the WWII Allies

---

* Go to ShopJBS.org to find several publications concerning the danger of the UN to American liberty.

as "the United Nations" without need of additional explanation, indicating that in mainstream thinking, the UN was a foregone conclusion even a year before coming into official existence.

The administration of Franklin D. Roosevelt worked to get support for a future international organization during the war and, as did the *Life* editorial cited above, many a newsreel stated that "United Nations" troops were landing on enemy-held beaches, when they were actually U.S. troops. So the American movie audiences were also being prepared. In September 1943, the Republican Party endorsed U.S. participation in a postwar international organization. In a now commonplace outcome, Republican grassroots opposition was neutralized by party leadership.

What became the UN General Assembly met in San Francisco in early 1945, and the U.S. Senate ratified the UN Charter on July 28, 1945, before the war in the Pacific was over. The UN came into existence in October 24, 1945, after 29 nations had ratified the charter.

Few Americans have actually read the charter — including those in Congress who ratified it. People should. Most feel after reading it that we should get out of the UN, since it cedes control over the use of our own armed forces to the UN Security Council. Any permanent member of the Security Council may veto the use of any member's armed forces, or even force any member to use their armed forces in combat.

The latter violates the Constitution of the United States, which states that only Congress can declare war, not the president or any treaty.

The five permanent members of the Security Council are the United States, Great Britain, France, *Russia*, and *China*. Ponder this.

Since becoming a member of the UN, the United States has

had very few years that we have not been at war, but we have never declared one during that time. All the wars have been based on UN Security Council resolutions. Russia and China could have, at any time, vetoed our involvement. Do we really want to put our nation's well-being and safety within the purview of foreign powers, especially those that are antagonistic to us?

In any case, *The Communist Manifesto* was setting the stage for the primary goals of the communists, including the future means to unite the Earth into a one-world government run by the communists. Or rather, it should be said, run by the secret cabal behind the communists. Sometimes, as is the case with free trade, the concept is couched in language which only reveals the true meaning upon close study and analysis.

Chapter Seven
Friends and Enemies

Marx spends a great deal of space in the *Manifesto* criticizing every movement at the time involved in some level of socialism and/or reform. Only the pure communist movement could be successful, in his eyes.

However, he also states that the communists would cooperate with certain movements from country to country, and names them. These movements no longer exist in the forms they did at the time the *Manifesto* was written.

Anyone who has studied the creation, advent, and supposed demise of the Illuminati will recognize many of these movements, since they were the offspring of Illuminism and/or its second-generation creation, the Carbonari. In the United States, the Carbonari was called Young America.*

It is only natural that Marx and Engels would defend and promote their particular branch of this overall conspiracy, communism, which remains to this day the main street-level organization which carries on the legacy of the master conspiracy.

Many have tried to emulate what communism has done, even while being enemies of communism — not so much because of what communism stands for, but because they want to be the

---

* For documentation of this fact, see *To the Victor Go the Myths & Monuments*, available at ShopJBS.org.

leaders of the movement and similar forms of government to fool the people into supporting them. After all, the same tactics and organization must be used if a group wants to control a country. They can call themselves anything they like; the end results must be the same.

The leaders of the two such movements that stood out the most in the last century were Hitler and Mussolini, developing forms of fascism which were almost the same as communism while rallying their people against communism. In fact, Mussolini was a co-conspirator of Lenin before developing his form of dictatorship.

Of interest to Americans, political leaders in the United States in turn used the methods *and words* of Mussolini to build their political base among the people. This was especially true of Franklin Roosevelt, who used Mussolini's words in his speeches, and the National Recovery Act (NRA), whose Blue Eagle campaign was a copy of Mussolini's economic program. The NRA was eventually ruled unconstitutional by the Supreme Court.

While Mussolini was originally a member of and leader within the Italian Socialist Party linked with Lenin, he fashioned a form of socialism to fit the need to bring the Italian citizens under his organization's control. The Black Shirts of fascism resembled the Carbonari under Mazzini and Garibaldi, who had just decades before united all of the boot of Italy under one flag. The basis for the Black Shirt organization, and the preparation of the people for fascist control, can be found in the work of the Carbonari over the preceding century. And, again, the Carbonari were the second generation of the Illuminati.

In Italy and Germany, part of the promotion of their forms of socialism was to present communism as so much of a threat that the people had to embrace fascism, a supposed enemy of communism. It was a Punch-and-Judy show. The same puppet master controlled the fighting puppets, to the delight of the audience. The conspiracy controlled both sides.

As an example, the main-street enemy of the Nazi brownshirts was Antifa, the communist street enforcers. The two groups often met head-on in the streets battling for control of meetings, events, etc. — and the streets themselves. Once the Nazis won, most of the members of Antifa joined the brownshirts because, other than the personality at the top (Hitler vs. Stalin), there was little difference between the philosophy and aims of the two groups.

The Germans came to refer to these former Antifa members turned brownshirts as "beefsteak Nazis": brown on the outside, red on the inside.

The same two movements went forward in American society, but since the American people were more free, were more educated in freedom's principles, had more exceptions to government regulations, and therefore were more resistant to government control, the socialists were less harsh or radical in presenting their proposals and how they were to be implemented. Nonetheless, the basic elements of the takeovers of Russia, Germany, and Italy were contained in the government programs of Herbert Hoover and, especially, Roosevelt's New Deal.

At the same time, communism was — and still is — presented as the enemy. The socialists promoted the idea that a little socialism would help forestall adoption of the more radical communism. Within American conservative circles, a growing movement (which became neoconservatism) started to promote a form of internationalism under "liberal" democracy to be a foil against international communism.

The result of the latter movement has been the growth of international alliances, which control our government outside of the Constitution and have goals closely resembling the aims of the communists in forming a one-world government — ostensibly in the name of fighting communism (or terrorism).

The American people have been bamboozled into creating a one-world government in the name of fighting communism. Yet, governmentally, the main goal of communism is a one-world government.

And, major steps toward this end have been made successfully under so-called conservative Republican leadership.

It was Richard Nixon and Henry Kissinger, recall, who "opened up" Communist China.

Then it was Democrats Zbigniew Brzezinski and Jimmy Carter who opened up trade and banking with that same Communist China.

Then back to Republicans again under the two Bush administrations. Indeed, George H. W. Bush said that his foreign policy objective was a New World Order, and he even published a booklet in August 1991 advocating the New World Order in those words: *National Security Strategy of the United States*, with the preface titled "A New World Order."

Then came the so-called collapse of communism in the USSR — nowhere else. In all of the Soviet satellites, the announcement was made that the communist parties would no longer rule their countries. No revolution. No upheaval. Just an announcement.

In none of these USSR satellite countries did the communist teachers leave the classrooms, the communist police resign, or the communist bureaucrats leave their desks and say they now had to find work in the private sector. There was no private sector, at least at first. And, most importantly, the communist-appointed judges remained in place.

Too many of the laws under communism remained. Some were altered, but few disappeared. No bill of rights — as we understand rights to be — was instituted. People in Europe can go to jail for maligning their president. We can call our president any fool thing we want to, but not in Poland or France, and certainly not in Germany, where political speech is tightly regulated and opposition parties are nearly outlawed.

What we are saying in this book is that, in the name of fighting communism, too much of the *Manifesto* has been and is being implemented in the United States, because people do not really understand the subtleties of Marxism.

And, that is the reason for this small volume. To create understanding of the words and intent of Marx and Engels. Their work was simply a codification of the efforts of evil men who came before them to so alter the thinking of the people in general — using an understanding of human nature — that the people would accept their own enslavement by the communists, and not understand how it was done to them until it was too late.

Some Americans are starting to wake up to the fact that something is terribly wrong. However, more people have to start figuring out just who their friends and enemies are.

The oath of office for officers and warrant officers in the U.S. Army reads like this:

> I, (name), do solemnly swear that I will support and defend the Constitution of the United States against all enemies, foreign and domestic; that I will bear true faith and allegiance to the same; that I take this obligation freely, without any mental reservation or purpose of evasion; and that I will well and faithfully discharge the duties of the office upon which I am about to enter, SO HELP ME GOD.
> DA FORM 71, JUL 1999

There are a couple of things which are very important about this oath. First, the potential officer swears he will support and defend the Constitution — the law of the land. He doesn't swear to defend the country or obey the president or the general staff. He swears to obey the Constitution.

Too often today, the young men taking the oath have not even studied the Constitution in their classes in school. They do not even realize to what they are swearing. In their mind it is their country, period.

He also swears to defend it from all enemies, foreign and domestic. Now, they tell him who the foreign enemies are. After all, he has to fight them, so he had better know who they are. But, they never tell him who the domestic enemies of the Constitution are.

A good place to start learning who these people are is to look in the halls of Congress. There are many enemies of the Constitution there. Even those who profess to be constitutionally minded vote for things which are unconstitutional all of the time. It is very rare that a member of Congress votes 100-percent constitutionally.

Americans need to realize that they must oppose enemies of the Constitution without compromise. Compromise with the Constitution only leads to more government, more intrusive government, and eventually totalitarian government.

But most people want to "play nice." They don't have the stomach for standing up for the Constitution. However, even though they must be ladies and gentlemen, they cannot compromise with evil.

Name the last time that a compromise was made in politics which moved the dial back toward constitutional government. You can't. Compromise always moves government toward more socialism and communism.

The time for resolve is now.

Note also that the oath of office above has the last four words in capital letters. That is the way it is on the form. The officer is swearing in the name of God that he will keep his oath. This is so important that it is in caps. But, if the officer does not even realize what the oath entails, it is meaningless.

The means by which Americans can overcome the advancement of Marxism is by studying and understanding the basic documents of our country: the Declaration of Independence and the Constitution, which also contains the Bill of Rights.

The Declaration of Independence is in direct conflict with *The Communist Manifesto*. The communists want a one-world government. The Declaration states that we are to be an independent country. *The Communist Manifesto* wants to rid the world of God and recognize the state alone as the source of the citizens' rights. The Declaration of Independence states that it is God's will that we separate ourselves, and that our rights come from God.

Both of the main tenets of communism, a one-world government and the elimination of God, are in direct conflict with the Declaration's provisions. It is no wonder that the close study of the Declaration is rare in government schools today.

Chapter Eight
The Subtleties of Communism

We need to review a little history that is generally unknown. Because much of American history has been wiped clean of some very disturbing facts in our past, many historical figures have been lauded who do not deserve the praise they receive.

Engels admitted that the communist leadership was a secret one. In the United States, the communists have an open organization in the streets and a secret one behind the scenes. The *results* of this latter cabal can be visible, but rarely can observers see and identify *those who are part of it*.

Americans, increasingly submerged in absurdist socialist propaganda and taught lies about our history, are therefore largely unaware of the influence of socialists in early American history, both during the life of Karl Marx and after.

As a result, it is often very difficult for someone to accept, at first, the facts of true history when initially presented to them — they can seem too fantastic to be true.

Marxists have the ability to sell socialism in such a manner that not everyone sees through their beguiling verbiage. As an example:

> We believe that government, like every other intelligent agency, is bound to do good to the extent

> of its ability — that it ought actively to promote and increase the general well-being — that it should encourage and foster Industry, Science, Invention, Intellectual, Social and Physical Progress.... Such is our idea of the sphere of government.
>
> Horace Greeley, 1850, as quoted in *Horace Greeley and Other Pioneers of American Socialism* by socialist historian Charles Sotheran, published in 1892.

In other words, individual citizens will not decide on necessary improvements. The government — made up of those who profess not to be socialists but who agree with socialists — will decide the "correct" science and industry, which inventions will go forward and be utilized, and the "correct" intellectual, social, and physical progress.

This is the aspect of the *Manifesto* referred to as the "association" making decisions in Chapter Two and Chapter Four, and the death of the individual in Chapter Six.

Listening to Greeley's words, at first blush it may seem good for government to be involved. But, in order to accomplish the above, the government must build a bureaucracy, and they must take taxes from everyone to implement the ideas and fund the bureaucracy — at which time the bureaucracy then controls everything. Invention is actually stifled under government, since invention requires the freedom to think outside of the box. It is freedom *from* bureaucracy that leads to invention. This is why America has been more inventive than any other country — because it has been more free.

At a minimum, the ideas above outlined by Greeley represent fascist socialism, a welding of government and business called *corporatism* today.

The process involves government planning, which leads to

full-scale socialism, then communism — the ultimate goal. This is inevitable and inescapable. Government planning appears to be so benign that the average citizen cannot imagine where the process will lead and what its ultimate end will be.

Planning by government means the death of individualism and property rights in all forms: personal, intellectual, and landed. Through planning, government will assume control over all or part of these in order to move its plans forward, through zoning, building projects, eminent domain, changes in society, and more. It means the death of all individual rights and liberty. If you lose the ability to control these matters, you lose the ability to control your future as well as your means to survive as an individual, and become dependent on the state as a result.

The point is that when the American people, or any people, are ignorant of the facts and basic lessons of economics and history, they can be manipulated. This manipulation always leads to more government to be used by the manipulators.

Horace Greeley was the publisher of the *New-York Tribune*, which had the largest circulation of any Sunday edition in the country. Its influence was profound. Greeley had several socialists on his editorial and writing staff, including Karl Marx, who wrote for the paper from Europe for 11 years prior to and shortly into the Civil War.

Indeed, the socialist/communist network helped build the paper's circulation.

Through the American Union of Associations, Greeley was a leader in forming nearly 50 communist communes prior to the Civil War. Once the commune movement started to wane, most of the members registered with the Communist International, as did Greeley himself, according to Charles Sotheran.

Greeley served in Congress, and was elected with everyone knowing what he stood for. He later ran for president against Ulysses

Grant on the Democratic and Liberal Republican Party tickets at the same time, but lost. It was not the first time a communist ran for president on a major ticket, and it would not be the last.

The communist organization used its tremendous political influence to get Greeley nominated on a major ticket, and capitalized on the ignorance of the American people, who did not understand the ramifications of such a candidacy.

People were losing their appreciation for and understanding of private property rights, not only in land but in intellectual property as well. While the process was subtle, the idea that government could control thought and invention was beginning to take hold.

In addition, the country was experiencing a large influx of immigration. The newly arrived people eventually voted, but a sizable number of them were not property owners so had little interest in property rights. Also, many of these immigrants were already oriented toward socialism, having fled Europe due to the failure of communist revolutions. It wasn't simply famine at home or the opportunity in America which drove them here.

The problem initially was not so much that of government getting directly involved in the intellectual process of the country, as much as it was the concerted efforts by the Marxists to control it by subterfuge. This was accomplished by infiltrating intellectual organizations such as historical societies, publishing companies, newspapers, colleges, etc.[*]

Later the government got directly involved in controlling intellectual property. Because the control was implemented slowly, though, over a prolonged period of time, the people did not notice there was anything to be upset about. There was rarely any one major step which prompted the people to say, "enough is enough."

---

[*] Again, one of the best sources for this aspect of history is the book *To the Victor Go the Myths & Monuments*, available at ShopJBS.org.

There was, and is today, a concerted Marxist narrative underlying the efforts to control everything that is mass produced in education and media — news, science, and even religion. Any thoughts contradicting the "party line" are ridiculed and suppressed as much as possible. However, this suppression is becoming more difficult to sustain, since more people realize that they cannot trust the sources of information they have been relying on and are seeking alternatives. The aggressive censorship efforts and other totalitarian policies that came with Covid opened the eyes of many for the first time.

The best depiction of the idea of government taking away the right to even think — much less produce something as a result of thinking — is the book *1984* by George Orwell. In the book, "Big Brother" was always watching, and no one was allowed to think differently than the state, let alone do anything with those thoughts. The right to individual thoughts was eliminated.

This was largely accomplished using the "memory hole": News items, articles, and government positions from the past which ran contrary to the new party line were eliminated from the archives and never again allowed to see the light of day.

Orwell had worked with the communists before World War II. He knew of their plans and where they were going, and wrote fictional books with which to warn readers of the dangers of a communist world. *1984*, his most terrifying, is probably his most famous.

This process has begun in the United States, and even elsewhere around the world, with the control and censorship of the internet. Many are realizing this now with recent revelations of the controls over Twitter which became known once the company was sold to Elon Musk. However, Musk is not what one would call a conservative, placing a globalist in charge of Twitter — once he had control — which subsequently changed its "name" to X.

Videos and articles which can substantiate constitutional and anti-communist arguments and writing have a habit of disappearing from the internet, or they get buried so deep in the system that it takes many difficult searches to ferret them out.

Many who have not felt the sting of censorship may not know just how extensive this online censorship is. And, it has been happening at the insistence of the government and with the collusion of private companies, who were coached by the government on compliance. This should not be mistaken for a new phenomenon, as government has long sought to force the media to be its servant. The CIA since its inception has had a program of influencing our citizens through the media, originally called Operation Mockingbird. This operation was supposedly stopped, but hints indicate its continuation in other forms.

Outside the United States, the Chinese communists have somewhere between 50,000 and 100,000 hackers that work for the People's Liberation Army. This can be verified by an online search for the subject of the 54th Research Institute of the PLA, and especially PLA Unit 61398 — if these have not yet been censored from the internet.

Not only do the Chinese hackers steal secrets from the militaries of various countries, they steal industrial secrets as well. They are also involved in shutting down websites or information they deem adverse to the Communist Party line.

In addition to hacking websites, they force companies to censor online content if they want to do business in China, a huge internet market. Many Hollywood productions, for example, have been censored in compliance with Chinese government demands in order to be screened there.

Technology news website *CNET* reported on one notorious example. Writing for that site in 2019, Jennifer Bisset recounted MGM's encounter with Chinese censors in 2012.

"MGM discovered China's sensitivity the hard way," Bisset recounted. "Its 2012 remake of alternate-history Cold War film Red Dawn depicted Chinese soldiers as enemies. After unhappy state-run Chinese media got hold of a leaked script, the company spent $1 million digitally editing out any evidence of the soldiers, shuffling in North Koreans instead."

Because of the threat of Chinese sabotage, the Trump administration outlawed the use of Chinese equipment in the United States from companies such as Huawei, and many other countries followed suit. Such policies were enhanced by law by Congress in 2021.

Internet services comply with Chinese censorship policies even within the U.S. if they want to continue doing business in China. In addition, such services as Google and Facebook are corporate members of the Council on Foreign Relations, and many of the high-level officers are members as well, so they must agree with the goal of a New World Order.

Freedom of speech includes individual intellectual property, which is increasingly coming under attack.

All of this follows the *Manifesto's* goal, with the field of communications gradually being placed under the control of the state.

Politicians understand the people are frustrated with the problems of private property rights, excessive taxation, etc., and use such frustration to enlist voter support for their candidacy or political party. They rarely, however, remedy the problems, since secretly the key leaders are closer to Marxism than they want the voters to realize.

One party talks a lot and moves left. The other party talks about the problem and does nothing.

Talk is cheap, as they say.

Chapter Nine

Immigration

Immigration, both legal and illegal, into the United States is a problem.

There is no country in history in which massive immigration hasn't changed the government of that country simply by the means of the native population being overwhelmed. This is not something taught in our schools, so most people do not think of the problem in this way.

The primary example in the ancient world was the influx of the Visigoths into Roman territory, and ultimately their taking and sacking of Rome. It would not have ever happened if the Roman government had not allowed the Visigoths to settle along the Roman border and invited many of them in, or had had sufficient legions in place to stop them. There were political aspects of this debacle, but this is generally the story.

Americans are concerned about the massive number of immigrants into America from all over the world, including the poor, the sick, and even potential terrorists in their ranks. The education of these people relative to what constitutes liberty is also greatly lacking. Immigration is in the millions annually, and over time constitutes many tens of millions of people.

In February 2024, Fox News reported: "Nearly 7.3 million migrants have illegally crossed the southwest border under President Biden's watch, a number greater than the population of 36 individual states."

Many people think in terms of these and other immigrants eventually voting for Democrats. This is too simplistic.

Immigration at one time meant that you had to have a source of support, a sponsor or some other means where you would not be a burden on the taxpayers. Those days are gone when it comes to those crossing over into the United States. Today, they *are* a burden to the taxpayers.

While the recent influx is concerning to people, the magnitude of the problem is bigger than most realize. The number of illegal immigrants before 2020 has been estimated to be 40 million. Many of the studies which once were on the internet quoting this number have disappeared over the last few years. For many years, the "official" number was 11 million, and it stayed that way for two decades even while millions were crossing the border. Post-2020, some pundits think the Fox News estimate is too low and place the number closer to ten million during the first three years of the Biden administration.

What is the Marxist position on this?

The *Manifesto* says this concerning their position:

> The Communists are further reproached with desiring to abolish countries and nationalities.

This says it all. We could leave it at that, except that modern changes facilitating the making over of our country are wrapped up in the issue of immigration — though most Americans are unaware of them.

The *Manifesto* goes on:

> The working men have no country. We cannot take away from them what they have not got. Since the proletariat must first of all acquire political supremacy,

must rise to be the leading class of the nation, must
constitute itself the nation, it is, so far, itself national,
though not in the bourgeois sense of the word.

National differences, and antagonisms between
people, are daily more and more vanishing, owing
to the development of the bourgeoisie, to freedom
of commerce, to the world-market, to uniformity in
the mode of production and in the conditions of life
corresponding thereto.

When you weld these words to those Marx has said about
free trade, you see that what he is referring to is a massive
change relative to borders and countries. Note, he says that
the proletariat must constitute itself a nation, but not in the
bourgeois sense of the word. In other words, he wants a
worldwide "nation," i.e., a one-world government made up of
communists.

How could this be accomplished? We see that so-called free
trade can tie up nations into alliances which lead to mergers as a
step-by-step means to merge all countries of the world into the
United Nations.

Another means is to eliminate borders and allow the free
flow of peoples into other countries.

This is what is happening to the United States.

Politicians who do nothing about the influx of immigrants
want them to come into the country. Many of them talk a good
talk, but they really do not fight, they just talk. Both political
parties are to blame; the fault is not with one party over another.
The political battles we see happening relative to immigration
are more Punch-and-Judy shows than most realize.

Let us quote John Adams in regard to political parties
opposing one another:

> There is nothing I dread so much as a division of the republic into two great parties, each arranged under its leader, and concerting measures in opposition to each other. This, in my humble apprehension, is to be dreaded as the greatest political evil under our Constitution.

> Letter to Jonathan Jackson, October 2, 1789

But, what if both political parties are only pretending to oppose one another, using rhetoric to keep their voters in line while the leaders of the parties have the same ends in mind? One party runs toward the goal, the other walks.

There is a great deal of evidence that this is the modern case, and many books have been written exposing this problem. There have been good men and women in both major parties, but on the whole the party apparatuses have been subverted by a secret cabal which has pushed forward the Marxist plan for America. One does it rather openly today, the other moves in that direction while talking otherwise.

To understand this problem, we recommend two books: *To the Victor Go the Myths & Monuments*, and *In the Shadows of the Deep State*, both by this author. The first documents the history of this cabal during the first one hundred years of America and the origins of the two major political parties. The second documents the influence of the Council on Foreign Relations on America in recent history.[*]

The goal of the Marxists is to wipe out the distinction of any borders, first in North America, then within the Western Hemisphere, and finally all around the world. One world. Run by them.

In Europe, they have succeeded in consolidating Western and

[*] Available from ShopJBS.org.

Central Europe into the European Union. They would like to bring Ukraine into that union as well, and they have created the conditions necessary to kick off a bloody war involving Russia to that end. Communist strategy, it will be recalled, uses war to build the interests of the communist world state, and this is exactly what is happening over the blood and tears of the people dying on the front and in the cities of Ukraine today. As a result of this war, Finland and Sweden have been brought into NATO, and much debate has swirled around the prospect of even Switzerland giving up its neutrality — and thus its independence — in the future.

Why would we see businessmen, professional politicians, and even clergy getting involved in this plan? Isn't it against their self-interest? It would seem so until we understand that the real end in sight is the building of power.

Power is more important than ownership, since it can be used to rule.

Mao, Stalin, Hitler, etc., were all poor men. For them, money, when they needed it, was only a means to an end. Once they had power, they didn't need money any longer. And, they soon, or from the beginning, devolved into evil when it came to dealing with their enemies or those whom they simply didn't like.

Power is a strong aphrodisiac — not in a sexual sense, but in the sense that certain men crave power and will do anything to achieve it. They are psychopathic megalomaniacs. Morality is left by the side of the road on their way to achieving power.

They will cooperate with one another to create the conditions for power. They usually end up fighting one another to make it look as if they are on different sides, but in reality it is show business — once again, Punch and Judy. The only real argument is who will be the ruler.

It takes a great deal of reading and searching to figure out who is trustworthy.

In general, it is necessary to trust but verify. It is not prudent to place complete confidence in people in power today, no matter what they say. Action speaks louder than words. So does inaction.

For instance, if former Speaker of the House Kevin McCarthy is such a good conservative, as some have insisted, why did he march with a man who had a long history of communist involvement his whole life, calling him his friend? We are talking about Congressman John Lewis.

Back to the point: Massive immigration is a part of the platform of Marxism. One side supports it openly, the other slow-walks its opposition — at least those in the leadership do. Why? We leave it up to you to answer.

Chapter Ten
Conclusion

So, we have seen how *The Communist Manifesto* threatens our freedom today. Now, what can be done to overcome the influence of the *Manifesto* on today's America?

First of all, one has to assume the responsibility to *do something*, not just talk about it. In general, this a problem in modern America: the lack of responsibility. It manifests itself in a variety of ways. Sometimes people rely on government to provide for themselves and their families in a variety of ways. Sometimes people stick their heads in the sand and refuse to get involved, refusing to acknowledge what is wrong.

The biggest problem we have is that people today do not assume the responsibility to work for good government, perhaps because they do not know what to do or how to do it.

Many conservative individuals want to be left alone, to be able to work, raise their families, enjoy life as they please, and mind their own business. They eschew joining organizations — they either do not want to spend the time, do not see an effective group, or do not understand the necessity of being organized.

Marxists are collectivists, and grouping together into organizations is a natural thing for them. But for conservative individualists, group think and group action are often tiring and occasionally repugnant. As a result, conservatives are hard to organize simply because they are individualists. As they say, it's like herding cats.

Yet as bad as the Marxists' philosophy is, especially in practice, they are winning simply because they do organize. That organization usually isn't visible, except when it is in the streets. The real organization works behind the scenes, often utilizing people who are not obviously part of the Marxist organization: the secret cabal as described by Engels.

Letting "George do it" hasn't worked out for those who oppose Marxism.

Effective opposition to the communist totalitarian scheme can only come about by getting people who believe in the U.S. Constitution to band together in an organization dedicated to working together to preserve freedom, good government, and national independence.

But what kind of organization?

First, it has to be strictly constitutional, not "conservative."

Second, it must stand for godly morality.

Third, it has to be organized right down to the neighborhoods, yet be a national organization working in concert on an agenda to counter the communist agenda, looking to the long run rather than simply getting involved in the issue of the day.

No single issue will save our country. Those standing against the communist program must have a robust counter agenda.

Since the goal of the communists is to use the United Nations to entrap the United States in a world government, then a movement to *Get US Out!* of the UN must be part of the freedom agenda.

Since it is the goal of the communists to do away with local police run by local citizens through their city councils and form a national police force in their place, which then would become part of the UN, a movement must be instituted to Support Your Local Police — *And Keep Them Independent!*

The same is true of the environmental movement, the schools, and more. As to education, even if you do everything else possible to save our country, if the schools keep churning out ignorant, even Marxist-oriented graduates, then something has to be done about the schools.

The organization must welcome all people to membership regardless of ethnic or religious background, and be concerned only with good character.

There is more, but you get the point. The only organization which has such an agenda and organizes people all over the country is The John Birch Society. In addition, the Society is the only organization which has a professional field staff across the nation to help grow the organization, train it, mentor it, and monitor it.

The John Birch Society has over 60 years of experience fighting Marxism. It has achieved many victories over the years, and has slowed down the agenda and timetable of the Marxists by at least 70 years. The biggest problem the Society has is that it is not large enough. Part of the problem of growing the Society is that the Society only wants people who are willing to do something, not simply join and pay their dues.

So-called conservatives must assume their responsibility to actually get involved. If the early Americans had the attitude of simply wanting to be left alone, we would never have had the War for Independence and the formation of the United States. Enough of them assumed their responsibility to get involved.

As John Adams said, it was a change in their attitude and responsibility which led to the War for Independence. If they merely were aware of what was wrong but did nothing about it, and took no responsibility, we would not have America as we know it today.

Overall, it did not take that many people during the Colonial period to get involved and save the day, and the situation is the same today. It only takes about three percent of the people to actually get involved to make a dramatic, positive impact.

More than three percent agreed with the American Revolution at the time, but only three percent actually did something. Three percent *actually getting involved* today will save our heritage of liberty.

Now that you understand, at least in part, *The Communist Manifesto* and its goals, isn't it time to get involved?

We are not talking simply about saving our country — we are talking about the future of our children and grandchildren. We have a responsibility to them.

> When bad men combine, the good must associate, else they will fall, one by one, an unpitied sacrifice in a contemptible struggle.
>
> Edmund Burke

Index

How Can I Make a Difference?

GETTING STARTED IS AS EASY AS 1,2,3

1 **Sign up for JBS news and action alerts**
- Stay informed with free content
- Visit www.JBS.org/e-newsletter to sign up now

2 **Contact your elected representatives**
- Local, state, and federal officials represent you
- Visit www.JBS.org/act-now for contact information

3 **Join The John Birch Society**
- National concerted action multiplies your impact
- Visit www.JBS.org/join to apply for membership today

The John Birch Society

P.O. Box 8040
Appleton, WI 54912-8040
(920) 749-3780 • **JBS.**org

"Less government, more responsibility,
and — with God's help — a better world."